Love Nishi

Anjali Sinha

Published by Anjali Sinha, 2021.

WELCOME!
About The Author
Copyright Page
Acknowledgements

COPYRIGHT

---

1. http://canva.com

The letters:

"Papa, where were you the whole day, yesterday?"

He doesn't say a word. He glares at me. He just freaking stands there and looks at me with a vile, repugnant look that makes me want to throw up.

"Like glaring will solve all your problems in life, huh?" I shrug my hands in front of him, walking in the kitchen to make him a glass of lemonade.

"What does Rahul wants now?" His face is filled with a vengeance.

"Papa, bhaiya (Indian word for brother, or elder brother in general) called me, because he is sick for the last couple of days now. He's getting down with subsequent bouts of fever in the morning and he suddenly recovers in the evening. He told me to tell you to call him later."

"What can I do from here? You children just keep putting pressure on me! What do you think I can do for him?"

Everything. How about everything?

"How about starting to be there for us?" I mentally voice out my question slowly, savouring it. He glares at me again. I look at him frustrated, and then I take my leave. I find my blue, bedazzled diary lying on my bed, so, I open it to a subtle page and start scribbling. I need to vent out my feelings.

Dear Papa,

How many times can you get angry in a single day? Will your giving brother the cold shoulder will vaporise all of your problems? Or our problems? Do you know how difficult it is to tolerate your cold behaviour? Do you even try to know what it's like to have a father who's never there for you?

Bet you never had that.

We bet you never had a cold-hearted father who ignored you when you needed him the most.

Does pushing your kids away helps you sleep better at night? I guess so it does. Because why else you'll derive pleasure from doing such a hurtful thing!

You're such a sadist, father. An effing sadist.

Can you once try and fill in the shoes to be his mother? Our—mine mother? God, I'm sick. I'm sick of playing the mother in this god damned house. I'm neither your mother nor his. I feel trapped. It feels so difficult to breathe. My lungs and nostrils are stuffy and constricted and repulsed from the pressure you both put on me. Or even expect from me.

Why these expectations, huh? I feel like I'm wasting my life looking after you guys. Who will look after me? Have you ever thought about it? Who will, huh? Do you ever consider how I feel? Will you ever? Will you even think about me–for once?

Looking forward to getting these questions answered in the so much awaited after-life.

Love,

Nishi.

Hi, my beloved diary,

"Why I am everyone's emotional punching bag? Why do they push and pull and squeeze me all at the same time? Can't they find someone else to play the pacifier in between their fights? Or maybe another victim for their verbal assaults?"

"Why don't just everyone— I mean every freaking person— leave me alone?"

These were some of the questions going through my head at infinity km/hr. Constantly. I was mulling at them while I cleaned the clothes, tidied the house and washed the plates. I am getting tired of all of this. I am sick of always being in the middle— that connection between Papa and Bhaiya (brother). Dad loves to glare at me, and my brother loves to be a total asshole to me. And, I am their favorite Frisbee. Throw her around as much as you like. As much as you can manipulate her. Sorry, I'm cussing. I didn't mean to. But, whatever.

Rahul, my stupid brother, is condescending about everything that he got so much easier in life. Money, college, a future probably. Getting away from the house. Getting out of the house. Being around his friends. Going into the warm, loving environment of an educational institution. And, here I am. . .writing letters in my old, wrinkled diary to get my anger out and to vent my feelings. Because apparently, I have no one who will listen to my crap. Go life. So, I turn another crumpled, orange-hued page of my diary, eating instant ramen noodles with crispy wafers. I think I've left a few too many bits of oily snacks, and orange crumbles and spots on the pages of my diary. Don't judge me, yeah. It's a snaccident. It may not be even a word. But, yeah, who cares?

Dear Papa,

I'm here. I'm going to come straight to the point and cut to the throbbing questions in my mind. I know you wouldn't like to answer these, but that doesn't stop me from having this gut-twisting question that doesn't quench my sanity. So, as I said, I'm gonna come ahead and lay it all out on you. Here it goes:

"When will you ever stop the discrimination between my brother and me? Have you ever–even like once–thought about how it feels to be a daughter in a household that is misogynist and isn't afraid to play favourites? How does one get dealt a bad hand if one's body organs look different from the other?"

"Does your disparity have a basis other than sex? I mean it has to daddy. Maybe there's some other reason. Maybe I eat too much. Or maybe I laugh too loud. Maybe I disappoint you too much. Because I've done-and do all three constantly."

"Why did you have me when you don't like a girl as a child? Like sincerely daddy, I was better off as a seed of your pleasure that didn't come into existence. You just didn't have to have me."

"Why did you bring me into this world? This question has terrorised, echoed in the deep crevices of my mind through all those nights when I wet my pillows with red eyes thinking about what I've done wrong. Was I just wrong to be a girl in this world full of lust? Is this why you hate me? Am I an object?"

"Why everything is so easy to get in my brother's life? Why everything is so difficult in mine? Because you know, he gets a good college education, and what do I get, huh? More chores to do. More clothes to wash, more plates to clean, more things to keep in order and then tidy them. More nights I spend in the kitchen making dinners for you that you don't even love."

"Why didn't you let me move when I finished high school? Yeah, daddy, say, tell me, why didn't you? Didn't I get into a government school that handed me a scholarship? But you said no, and you just didn't say no. You forbid me. You forbid me to go into a different state and go to the best effing university in all of India because it didn't suit your ego and your living conditions. You forbid me like it's the fucking—yes, yes, I'm cussing, I can't contain my anger anymore— seventeenth century. How can you let your slave just be free? I feel like Dobby, waiting for a piece of cloth from his master."

"When you didn't let me move then? Huh tell me now why didn't you? You didn't have to pay for my education; you just had to pay a few bills for me, like a place to stay, even their dorms didn't ask you enough to pay. Have you thought about that? Have you thought about how your actions have bullshitted everything that contained my future? How everything, everything just turned into a big pile of ash and mortar and became my future? I will never go to college. There goes my dreams. Yes, daddy, you took my dreams and burned them with your bare, malice-filled hands."

"Will you let me move out of the house on my own in the future? Let me answer this for you, a hard, solid 'no'. I mean how could you, being you! It has to be a big no from your side."

"Why do you love controlling my life so much? Is it your personal favorite? Or your pastime? It must be. Because you love face-planting yourself into my life. Not letting me see my friends, not letting me go out even to buy groceries. Giving me the stink eye when it suits your vision. Harassing me and physically hurting me when it suits you. Yeah, so. Yeah, dad. I think you love controlling and possessing every part of my life."

News Flash: I hate living here. I really do. (In case, you haven't figured it out, yet. I also hope you pay for this. Someway. Somehow. I don't want to know which way. I don't want to know how or what or when. I just would like you to feel the kind of loneliness I feel, walking through my house day in and day out. The kind of void that nothing fills.) Hope we can talk it all out. Someday. Probably. (My naive heart talking right here. Because my equally naive mind knows that we won't ever.) Looking forward to that day eagerly. Yes, I do look forward to the best things in life.

Like watching you shiver in your place while here I pinch my nails on my skin to feel if it's real. Whether that day ever comes or not.
Your unloved, unsympathetic daughter,
Love,
Nishi.

"I think my stomach is upset." Your voice rattles the empty living room area, which is seldom filled with the people I love.

Silence.

"Have you ironed my white shirt?" You keep going on, Papa, with no care of the world, or, in short, my world. You're only concerned about yours.

Silence.

"Bring me the dinner, will you?"

You are now walking up to my room, giving me orders like I'm some servant inside a mansion, held responsible for the up-keeping and the smooth running of the household, which I am. No voice crawls in the background. I silently place all the plates containing flatbread (rotis), vegetable curry, yoghurt and almond milk in front of him. I pour him a glass of water from the bronze jug on the dining table.

The meeting of the rough surface of the metallic jug reverberates with the jagged edges of the table—producing an eerie sound that describes all the melee around the house.

Silence.

Then, I saunter back into my room calmly. I slam the door shut, hoping it makes enough noise that it'll exceed the noises on the inside. My brain and heart are all over the place, vibrating like a tuning fork. There are some of those reluctant silent tears, brimming at the back of my tired, dark-circle curtained eyes. I try not to spill them. I command my brain to assuage the pain that I'm feeling. I don't need this right now. I tell my brain to deal with it. Just effing deal with it.

"Happy thoughts, okay, happy thoughts!" I mentally scream. I try not to surrender. But to no vain. Why did I think it's going to be any different? These things seldom help me. So, I pick up my diary which is lying sprawled on the green covers of my bed. I hold it close to my chest, tightening my grip on the book's skeleton. Maybe, I should write it all down. Yeah, it will take some of the sting away from all the bitterness that's enveloping my soul. When I'm ready after contemplating for a while, my pen starts pouring those burbling feelings and egging more tears on the white underlined page.

Dear Papa,

It pains me really to give you the silent treatment. I know I'm eighteen years old, and it's too late in life to be acting like this. Am I too big to give you the silent treatment? Or, is it the other way round? Am I really so grown up? I can't believe it. I'm eighteen years old, but it still doesn't hurt any less. Because honestly I still have no control over my emotions. Or, feelings. Or anything, for that matter.

I thought when you grew old, you grew up. To be a rational human who makes better decisions or their brain works better in life. Alas! That doesn't happen, does it?

I'm still here, making the same mistakes that I've made in the past, over and over again. I can't control the way people make me feel. The way they affect me. I can't stop caring about you or my brother.

Isn't it the stark reality?

No one can control how the other person standing in front of them is feeling or thinking right in the passing moment. It does make me think though. About how it makes you feel. About how you really feel when you see big, glassy tears in my brown eyes. I'd want to know if it hurts or not. I'd really like to.

But sometimes. . .other questions tick in the back of my brain. I think and think and think about why you don't. Why you don't care? Isn't it an innate ability for parents to care about their child right from the moment they are born? Isn't it the right thing to do?

But. . .what is right or wrong really?

That brings me to me my next question.

Why is that that I'm the only one who cares?

Why can't I be just like you guys? Why couldn't I just un-care about everything related to you?

Is there a paradox hidden between the lines? Please tell me, if it is. Or, god intended it to be the way it really is. That you come alone in this world, with momentary caretakers—aka parents, and you die alone, love-less and lonely. Still. . .I'm going to tell you what I care about. You know what hurts the most. It's the fact that you don't care enough. And I'm always left thinking that I'm not good enough. It's difficult wrapping my head around this nauseating feeling that always threatens to spill right through my eyes or lungs. This is not good, Papa. Adding to that, no matter what I'll ever do, or the sacrifices I make, you'll never care. That's the realist version of my life. It'll be never enough.

Nothing. I'll. Ever. Do. I'm. Not. Enough. Good. Bad. Whatever.

And after all my inquisitive musings, I'll let you in one of my deepest insecurities of all, I'm scared that you feel the same.

Your daughter who's trying to un-care about you and your son,
Love,
Nishi.

I held my pinkie toe in between my thumb and the index finger, crying. There's a huge gash on my toe that's only flushing out blood. The rest of the toe has swollen up to the size of a pea. The swelling had just started to change into pink. I can't wait to see it change into purple. There's like a palette of colour transformation going on right in front of my eyes, and I don't know if I'm so deranged to be curious or excited about it. Because, holy mother of the lord, it hurts a lot. I sob silently taking deep breaths, my chest heaving slowly with anger. I mean I'm angry yeah, about a lot of things. But you would probably know a lot on that. Because that's all I do. Complain. Sit and fuss about all of it. Like a sixty years old, senile old woman who has seen more sad days than happy ones. And, that bites me. Like really hard. It saddens me. About how depressed I am. And there's no one to extinguish my pain and pop the balloon of my sadness. I don't even have nobody who cares. And... it's just mother-effing sad.

Why no one is ever here to know my pain? Is my pain of a different kind than the others?

No one is ever here to tell me it's okay. That's it okay to feel like shit sometimes. That it's okay to fuck up and not give so many shits about it. That life is full of meaning when you really decide to love it. To live it. Nobody is ever here to hold my hand and tell me that I'll get through this.

"It'll be okay." I say to myself.

"It'll be okay," I reassure myself.

I hobble and jump on one foot somehow making it to the refrigerator, looking for some ice. The pain intensifies when I accidentally stub it again with the left ajar door of the fridge. I squeal and yelp, and hobble back to my couch. I notice the blood on my kitchen floor making a line of direction to my dark couch. It feels like I'm leaving a guideline in blood for some monster to follow and eat me in one bite. Maybe a piranha.

Oh! Now it's bleeding as it has never before. Like someone has turned on a faucet. Jesus holy Christ.

I mumble certain unfamiliar profanities under my breath. I curse the damn refrigerator, its damn door and my damn life. I hate it when it's lonely. I hate it how always no one's there for me. How lonely it gets when I'm trying to pick myself back up but need someone to help me glue back the pieces. How lonely and dark it gets when no one is even there to take care of me when I'm sick and hurting. I think no one deserves that kind of loneliness. Some of the days, I cry about it. Some of the days, I move on with my life. I mean what else I can do about it. Those are the cards that I've been dealt with in my life. I think I should accept it. Probably it will hurt a lot less.

"What else I can do about it?" I ask the universe.

Nothing.

Nothing is in my effing control. It never was. I wash the gushing wound with some quick, flowing tap water and put some antiseptic liquid-Dettol on it, cursing the holy origin of the water. I loop myself back to the bed and turn a new page in my old, loving diary.

Dear Papa,

Hello, I guess. How are you? I think it's been enough of the 'me giving you silent treatment' that is.

I hope you're happy. I hope that you really enjoy not talking. It's already been three days since we last talked. I hope you appreciate my silence. I really do. You never say anything to break it. I hope you're enjoying it the way it is. I do think you're deriving pleasure from my silence. So, silence it is. I'm not here to complain, maybe— I hope you find it amiable that my left leg's pinkie toe is all sore and swelled up. It also bled a lot.

But you won't probably care. Why would you? It's not like you are hurt. It's not like you bled until you were nauseous. I guess you'll never want to know about it. Or, anything, in general.

I hope you're enjoying your evening out with your friends. I hope you enjoy talking to them, telling them how much of a sadist you are, and how less invested you are in your own children's lives. No? Oh, well. Was worth a try, daddy. I guess you find the weather lovely outside; since you've prohibited— forbid me, yeah that happens in India— your own daughter from stepping out or even going outside and do normal human things, such as enjoy walks. I hope you'll be happy from the inside— maybe a lot— when I someday self-harm or injure myself to the point of no return, and not even care enough to tell you. I hope you appreciate it all. I really do. Do I still sign as your unloved daughter? Oh, I forgot that you wouldn't care about this too!

Your daughter's swollen left pinkie toe that really, really hurts,

Love,

Nishi.

Dear beloved diary,

The past few days have been hysterical. I'm losing my mind. My home life has gone to shit. My relationship with my dad had been nothing but crappy. Most of the time, he doesn't even care if I live, breathe or eat. And if you ask me, that's a shitty position to be in. But you wouldn't know. . .would you? You can't feel the way I feel. You can't think the way I ponder. And, at the end of the day, I can't deny the fact that I'm lonely. So lonely.

When I'm cramming over my books, my father chooses to just saunter in my room, without knocking. Indian parents often do that. They don't know the first letter of privacy. It's kind of a foreign thing for them. Have been that way for decades.

Y'know, he didn't ask me anything, he went about his merry way and stopped in front of the large wooden chest. He doesn't look in my direction and just fumbles through things, then goes on to do something by the big wooden chestnut almirah, arranging some papers and some magazines strewn upon it. He fixes the mess, silently observing me through the long glass mirror.

I squirm slightly under his scrutinizing glare, but duck my face in concentration in 'How to kill a Mockingbird.' I make mental notes on how my father is dissimilar to the protagonist's father. Even when the protagonist and I have been through the same circumstances, how are lives have been exactly different? I parched for love, and she for attention.

What better ways to ignore your father than to divulge in pure concentration in literary fiction?

My head goes on and on. He takes some money out of his black trousers pocket, turn slightly towards the edge of my bed, silently placing it under my good old diary. He clears his throat for my undivided attention.

Lol. Parents.

They think money, gifts, toys, sweets can fix everything. We break the things we love the most. Sometimes, it's our children. Sometimes, we forget that our children are not things. That goes for the entire human existence on earth and other celestial planets.

"Here's some money for. . .that thing you wanted," he says tight-lipped, "keep it. If I don't need it for your exams, you can keep it all." He coughs at the end and gazes back in the mirror. I silently look at him and then back at my book.

Classic single parent move.

If only money solved it all. But it doesn't. Does it dad? He doesn't even know how to play the money card.

Geez.

I silently shake my head when he leaves my room. Probably in confusion about his awesome parenting skills. Because it still hasn't made me jump in glee, or have my face contorted in satisfaction. Most of all, it still hadn't made me talk.

Who knew not talking makes your father want to pay you? If I had known, I'd be a millionaire.

Love,

Nishi.

Sarcasm aside. I flip another page fetching an ink pen to scribble in my thick blue-green diary.

Dear Papa,

You are so awesome. No imagination there. Honestly. Sarcasm definitely and surely intended. Please believe that.

There's nothing left to not believe when it comes to you. You give me money when I don't ask for it. You don't listen when all I want is to talk to someone. People say love comes in the purest form in parents.

Where should I go and find that kind of love? In my friends or lovers? Because you don't know Papa, the kind of relationships out there are just dangerous or poisonous. Girls want to befriend you just to climb that social hierarchical ladder and boys, well boys. They just want to fuck with you.

And I'm not even kidding.

It's grimy and grisly out there. Do you even know what are the risks there are involved in leading a teenage life? Do you even understand? Are you seriously that thick? Are you seriously that emotionally challenged? Are you seriously lacking those genes of undefiant and unconditional love? Or is it some apocalypse's after-effects? That I obviously missed out on in my mother's womb.

No wonder, I'm messed up. Thanks to you.

I'm thanking you here for all the daddy issues that I live with and that I'll carry around for the rest of my life. My anger has vanished, you know. It takes a lot to be angry at you. Or anyone and anything, in general. I'm tired, dad. I'm just tired. I'm done. Sometimes, I wonder how can you make and keep me so unhappy. You are so much out of this world. Oftentimes in my darkest moments, I wonder if mom was also unhappy with you. Was she? Is this accurate much? Perhaps, I don't want to know all the answers. I would never have all those answers anyway.

Sincerely, I do hope your parenting skills improve. With time and my patience. I really hope you change or I will change drastically.

Love,
Your only daughter whom you so casually ignore,
Nishi.

These last few days have been no good. Life has taken various twists and turns and I've lost one of my childhood best friends this week. I still can't believe that she's gone. Just like that. I can't believe I was so engrossed in university examinations to even acknowledge. What a heinous thing I have done? How could I have done to such a thing to my dear friend? I'm beyond mercy.

She was the light in my life for so many years. She had saved me in so many ways where I didn't save myself.

I couldn't even open my heart to someone who has had looked out for me several times in the past. How sad is the fact that. . .you never really know what the other person is thinking? How you generally fail to be there for somebody whom you think the world of?

Sometimes, it's inevitable.

You can't really save everybody. But, that doesn't mean—god no, that we shouldn't try. We should. With everything we have in ourselves. To be the light of the person who's lost and treading in darkness. It's sometimes just overwhelming when you're dealing with a lot of your own problems, that you lose sight of your priorities and the responsibilities it brings.

But, as I said, you should always try. You can change lives if you try. And that's the one pattern, I'm seeing in my father lately. I don't want to jinx it, but he's trying lately. He is. He has started to take small steps. And I'm bloody positive. Cause you know, the small ripples in the sea can set an explosion of waves to the shore. I'm not waiting for an explosion but I think it's high time, a miracle happened. Goddammit, you know I deserve it.

PS— I miss you terribly, Neha.

Love,

Nishi

And as my ritual entails, I find my diary to get rid of my inner thoughts and positively jot them down as a therapy routine in journaling.

Dear Papa,

I see you. Don't worry. I see that you're trying. It's more than what I could've asked of you lately. It's not a lot but you're getting there. I'm positively surprised and it's kind of nice that you're making efforts, it's so much necessarily needed.

For the first time in forever, I saw you putting your dirty plates in the kitchen-sink after dinner. I was appalled. I caught my breath and looked back at my dinner. It set out a ripple of emotions in my chest. The kind of stuff that wreaks havoc in private.

I couldn't place a finger on that feeling, but now that I think about it, it must be hope.

After a long time, I feel like you're trying to understand. To work through our unsaid problems. Not to say, I silently forgave you.

I closed my eyes and looked over the hurt I've suffered in the past few months. That was such a daughterly thing to do, but like you, I'm trying. I want to heal. I want to work on our relationship. I want it to heal too.

I want to go back to those old days when as I hopped inside our home, the first thing I did was to take you by the finger and sat you down, and told you about everything that is going wrong in my life.

I want to be there again, Papa. Believe me, I want to go back to that happy child again, as we were back then. I know it's not easy. I know it will take a lot of time and healing but after a long while, I am willing to try.

That's why I broke the silence today. It needed to go.

It takes a lot of effort from me; to not speak, you know. It drains me. It leaves me enervated. You don't know how does it feel to not speak an entire day to the only person living with you inside the house. To smudge the inky darkness of silence with my long faded fingers. I won't promise that I won't give you the silent treatment again.

See, I can't do that. I can't let myself trust that blindly again. I don't believe in myself that way. But, I do promise to talk things out with you. I'll try. I'll try to wage the differences between us. I would persevere. I will try to make you feel comfortable enough to share with me. To talk about your own problems out with me. That's, once again, such a daughterly thing to seek for.

Personally, I hope you keep surprising me in the days to come. I would look out for those small changes that give me hope. Because that's all I've left right now. Don't let that die within me. Let that candle illuminate in this darkness of pain and grief. Hold my hand through everything again. I wish to get through these times, Papa.

Again, I hope you become the old parent you once were: a kind, loving and better father. I'll be hopeful and looking forward to that. I sincerely do, Papa.

Your loving and once-again-filled-with-hope daughter,

Love,

Nishi.

Hello to you my *confidant*,

My father has been a negative person all his life. He's the eternal cynical bastard and I'm the over-ly optimist daughter who was born in the wrong country at the wrong time. No, my country is not at war, but there are hostilities and resentment inside close doors which pervades into the life of young children, who are too young to make their own decisions. My father is a pathetic, controlling man who is as toxic as the nuclear, radioactive substances that leaked into the atmosphere during World War II. I have grown up in that kind of atmosphere. I have won some battles and have lost some of them. Honestly, I've lost more than I've won.

I've shunned people, memories, opportunities and great experiences in my life because my father was an obstacle in meeting them. I've continuously heard the word *no* as if it was the word God intended to swing by me before anything I was supposed to embark on. My rationality on things and people and circumstances have generated a moment of fake hope inside me, liberating me from the pain I was feeling in the moment. I needed a bit of light to get through the darkness evident in the closed spaces of my life. I sought normality rather than actuality.

How can you hold your own when you think the only parent you have, the only pillar of your substance is vehemently opposing you? How far will you go? Far or not far, I don't know. I've been a kid and I've been an adult both at the same time, still figuring out everything. I don't know how much of a good job I'm doing. Probably not the best but I don't let it hinder me in any way. I know how to adjust my sails once in a while when the tides are high. I want to get far in the ocean. I *need* to.

I'm still fighting and I will keep fighting. There's no stopping me but sometimes it feels good when the sun rays seep in a cold, dismal winter morning. It's perfectly okay when it doesn't but sometimes I need someone to hold my hand and tell me it's okay, you're doing fine.

Is that too much to ask? I think it is. I need to tell myself that. I need to get strong and reverent in things I do. Passionate about things and compassionate about people in my life. I need to stop using my father as an excuse to keep me back from my own personal growth. I need to grow. Far away from this suffocating environment but sometimes even lotuses bloom in the dirtiest, marshiest waters and I need to take a breath and let it be a lesson for the rest of my life.

People make decisions. And sometimes the hurt and the pain inflicted on you is because of those stupid, abhorring decisions but that doesn't mean you can't make anything out of it. Perhaps this is my optimism or my positive side speaking. I don't know, I'm still figuring this out too.

Until later,

Love,

Nishi.

Hi mummy,

I haven't written you a letter before. I have no idea why I haven't tried that. I have so many things to share and say to you. First of all, I'm quite mad that you never left me a string of letters like in the movie Kuch Kuch Hota Hai. Till I turned nine, every day I thought and prayed and hoped that a letter would just turn up on the door from some long distant aunt I've never heard of. But I was disappointed. How typical of me to start a letter to you complaining about something you never did for me? Are all daughters supposed to act this way towards their mothers?

Am I any different?

I'm so mad at you for leaving me alone in this world so young. I'm completely furious. I'm so mad that sometimes my blood burns at the thought of never seeing you again. I was never given a choice. I never chose you to go to another state to get that fucking transplant. I wish you never went. But I could also see the pain you had to go through. . .every fifteen days with that dialysis machine digging holes in your arms. I wish I could've done something. I wish I could've taken some of your pain away, mummy. I wish you somehow managed to handle all that you were handling and stayed on till the medical advancement reached all corners of India. Do you know now people with different blood-types can give their kidneys without worrying that the patient's body will definitely reject the kidney?

I read your organ transplantation books.

I read your poetry and romance books, the fantasy ones and all of Amrita Pritam. That's all I have left of you. All I have now is a couple of your books because the young me was too hurt to keep all of your books. It all reminded her of you. I couldn't bear looking at another book with your name signed on the front knowing that's the last time you'll ever sign your name on a paperback. It was just too hurtful, mummy. I missed you too much. I still miss you. The pain, the ache, the throbbing of the heart has still yet to leave me, even after more than a decade. When does losing your mum becomes easier?

I've reached all the milestones in my life without you: I grew my hair out for the first time after you were gone, I had my periods, I had my first real crush, I fell in love, I fell out of love, I graduated high school, I became a writer, I got my first job, I went to university, I got my first real job that paid a lot, I fell in love again, I fell out of love again, I got depressed and just the wheels keep turning, ma, I just wish you could be here watching the cogs running with me.

I sometimes wish I knew you. I only have tids and bits and some flashbacks here and there about how you were to me. I don't ever remember you being cruel. I do remember you yelling at me a couple of times but that's because of my mistakes but I also remember your tenderness, ma, the way you would put a cold washcloth of my hot face, the way you cradled my head after I had split it open, the way you would pat my stomach to put me to bed. Can I have it all back just for one day?

I sometimes wish it didn't hurt so much. I never knew how to grieve you because when you left me I was a small child. That just means I have to grieve you my whole life. Nobody is ever going to be you and that's the bitter truth I've come to learn. I'll never have the love of a mother for as long as I shall live and I don't know if it'll just be a gaping hole in my chest that I'll never know how to fill.

Papa still doesn't know how to talk about you. It's perhaps because he never got over you. I don't know if he even wants to. I just see a mountain of his grief tucked way deep inside his chest. He doesn't know how to even mention you or your name in conversations. It has been more than 17 years now, but he still has a huge picture of you on the wall right next to the place where he sleeps. I don't think he even knows how to process his grief. But I do want him to work on it. He's quite unhappy, ma. Also, lonely. I wish him healing and companionship.

He doesn't deserve to grow old without someone. I wish he processed his feelings and got out of the old way of Indian thinking and started his life new someplace else. I wish he opened himself up. To me or to someone else.

Bhaiya is the same way. Like father, like son. He remembers more about you. But he is afraid to recall and remember and think about things and conversations. He was 9 when you left him. I think it's too painful for him. He misses you a lot. He's not a grownup by any means still. He has a lot of growing up to do, ma.

I think Papa did the best he could. In his own fucked up ways, he did what he knew, he did what he had seen, he did what he thought was right. I forgive him for so many things and I will continue to do so. I know that somewhere deep inside him resides a father that he was to me before you passed away. When you were gone, it completely changed him. It changed all of us. He was mad for a lot of years. To think about it now, he still is. But he tried.

He didn't leave us like your family, ma. Now, everyone from your family calls after letting me and bhaiya down so many times. They want to know us. It burns my skin. We didn't deserve all those years when they mistreated us. I wish they would go away. I wish your mom never calls me again. I wish your brother and his entire family never calls up Papa or me or Bhaiya again. I'm tired of their faking everything, and their fake concern and their fake love. I just never want to see them ever again.

My small family needs to heal away from your former family's bad energy. I've seen all of their true faces so young in my life, that I'm sometimes scared about what true humanity is like. So much negativity and hatred.

I will always love you, though. I wish you were more loved when you were on this Earth and I wish someone loved you more than your family ever loved you. Maybe Papa did that once. But now, I'm here to love you from a distance. I just hope wherever you are, you are happy and content.

Love,
Your daughter,
Nishi

Preorder Anjali's next book:

Https://www.amazon.in/Miles-Within-Constellations-love-does-nt-ebook/dp/B08ZVQ6B7R/ref=sr_1_1?dchild=1&keywords=miles+within+constellations+anjali+sinha&qid=1616749056&sr=8-1

About The Author

Anjali Sinha is a journalist and a content developer and strategist who romanticises book characters too much. She fell in love with books when her mum bought her first story-book in grade 1. She loves cookies and new cities and philosophical conversations with optimism. She is constantly found nestled under her duvet making stories up in her head.

Find her on Instagram: @authoranjalisinha

Find her artist Insta: https://www.instagram.com/anjalifromy-
outube/

Find her on Radish: @anjalisinha

Find her on Wattpad: @anjalisinha

Find her on Twitter: https://twitter.com/AnjalisinhaWp
Find her on Linkedin: https://www.linkedin.com/in/theanjalisin-
ha/
Find her on Facebook: https://www.facebook.com/authoranjalisin-
ha/?eid=ARB7YfSXntC_Px3e6Z3LcTD9OLxsVVH-
bCbv_l_hkG4ky_kh4w2pr_0rPSnZmM3bgx4M1CjVEBpwHEmnI
Join The Meltdown fam: https://www.facebook.com/themelt-
downmag

Mail her on gmail for queries, or to share feedback:
anjalisinha666.as@gmail.com

Acknowledgements

This book is something I wrote back when I was 16 on Wattpad. I was dealing with more things than what I had the courage to bear. I was lonely and hurt. This book was my safety blanket on the internet. It gave me the determination to keep on moving.

The reason I'm posting this on the internet is so that some other 16-yr-old can find refuge in it. I hope it becomes your safety blanket.

Thank you for reading!

I loved having you read this book!

Don't miss out!

Visit the website below and you can sign up to receive emails whenever Anjali Sinha publishes a new book. There's no charge and no obligation.

https://books2read.com/r/B-A-QSWL-XEGNB

BOOKS 2 READ

Connecting independent readers to independent writers.

Also by Anjali Sinha

Loving You
Loving You

THE MELTDOWN SERIES
The Meltdown
The Meltdown Jan 2021 Edition

Standalone
Love Nishi